# WIFE

# WHAT SHE SAYS
# VS
# WHAT SHE
# REALLY MEANS

If you enjoyed a good laugh while decoding the mysteries of marriage, I'd love to hear from you!

© Walter Goodwin
All rights reserved

*What She Says:*

**"I'm fine."**

*What She Really Means:*

**"I'm definitely not fine, and I'm not in the mood to explain."**

*What She Says:*

**"Do whatever you want."**

*What She Really Means:*

**"You better not do what you're thinking."**

*What She Says:*

## "We need to talk."

*What She Really Means:*

## "You're about to hear something you won't like."

*What She Says:*

**"I guess it's okay."**

*What She Really Means:*

**"It's really not okay, but I don't want to fight."**

*What She Says:*

## "I'm not mad."

*What She Really Means:*

## "I'm furious, but I'm waiting for you to figure that out."

*What She Says:*

**"You don't have to get me anything."**

*What She Really Means:*

**"You better get me something thoughtful."**

*What She Says:*

# "It's up to you."

*What She Really Means:*

# "It's not up to you. Do what I want."

*What She Says:*

# "Do you like this outfit?"

*What She Really Means:*

# "Tell me I look amazing, or else."

# "Nothing's wrong."

*What She Really Means:*

# "Everything is wrong, but I want you to notice without me saying it."

*What She Says:*

## "I'll be ready in five minutes."

*What She Really Means:*

## "You've got at least 30 more minutes to wait."

*What She Says:*

## "It would be nice if..."

*What She Really Means:*

## "I want this done immediately, but I'm trying to be polite."

*What She Says:*

## "Can we talk later?"

*What She Really Means:*

## "I need time to calm down before I explode."

*What She Says:*

# "I don't care where we eat."

*What She Really Means:*

# "You better choose my favorite place, or you're in trouble."

*What She Says:*

## "Go have fun!"

*What She Really Means:*

## "You better not have too much fun without me."

*What She Says:*

## "You don't listen to me."

*What She Really Means:*

## "You didn't hear what I needed you to understand."

*What She Says:*

**"Let's just drop it."**

*What She Really Means:*

**"I'm not over it, and we're definitely not dropping it."**

*What She Says:*

# "I'm not hungry."

*What She Really Means:*

# "I'll just eat all of your food instead."

*What She Says:*

## "You never help around the house."

*What She Really Means:*

## "I need you to start helping right now."

*What She Says:*

**"I don't care."**

*What She Really Means:*

**"I care a lot, but I'm not saying it directly."**

*What She Says:*

**"I'm going to bed."**

*What She Really Means:*

**"Come to bed with me, or I'll be annoyed."**

# "Do you think she's pretty?"

# "If you say yes, you're in deep trouble."

*What She Says:*

## "I'll take care of it."

*What She Really Means:*

## "I don't trust you to handle it, so I'll do it myself."

*What She Says:*

# "Maybe we should just forget about it."

*What She Really Means:*

# "I'm letting this go, but don't do it again."

**"I'm not upset."**

*What She Really Means:*

**"I'm very upset, but I don't want to talk about it... yet."**

*What She Says:*

# "It's not a big deal."

*What She Really Means:*

# "It's a huge deal, and you better fix it."

*What She Says:*

# "I don't need any help."

*What She Really Means:*

# "Please help me, but I don't want to ask."

*What She Says:*

## "I don't mind."

*What She Really Means:*

## "I mind a lot, but I'm testing your awareness."

# "Sure, you can go out with the guys."

# "I hope you know this is a trap."

*What She Says:*

**"You always say that."**

*What She Really Means:*

**"I'm tired of hearing this, and you need to change it."**

*What She Says:*

## "We'll see."

*What She Really Means:*

## "No, we won't see. I've already made up my mind."

*What She Says:*

# "Let's not argue about this."

*What She Really Means:*

# "We're definitely going to argue, and this isn't going to end well for you."

*What She Says:*

## "I don't want to bother you."

*What She Really Means:*

## "I want to bother you, but I'm waiting for you to offer help."

*What She Says:*

# "I just need some space."

*What She Really Means:*

# "You need to apologize and make it right."

*What She Says:*

# "It's fine, I'll do it myself."

*What She Really Means:*

# "You should have done this already, and now I'm upset."

*What She Says:*

## "I'm just tired."

*What She Really Means:*

## "I'm emotionally exhausted, and we need to talk."

# "Do you even care?"

*What She Really Means:*

# "I need you to show me you care right now."

*What She Says:*

## "It's nothing important."

*What She Really Means:*

## "It's very important, but I don't want to say it first."

*What She Says:*

## "I don't want to talk about it."

*What She Really Means:*

## "I want you to push me to talk about it."

*What She Says:*

## "You're right."

*What She Really Means:*

## "You're definitely not right, but I don't feel like arguing anymore."

*What She Says:*

**"I'm not a fan of surprises."**

*What She Really Means:*

**"I love thoughtful surprises."**

*What She Says:*

**"Just give me five more minutes."**

*What She Really Means:*

**"I'll be done when I'm done. Don't rush me."**

*What She Says:*

## "You pick the movie."

*What She Really Means:*

## "Pick the movie I want, or we're switching it immediately."

*What She Says:*

## "Let's just agree to disagree."

*What She Really Means:*

## "We can agree, but I still think I'm right."

# "You're such a great listener."

# "You're listening now, but where were you the last 10 times?"

# "I'm not feeling well."

# "I need attention, sympathy, and maybe some pampering."

*What She Says:*

# "Can you do me a favor?"

*What She Really Means:*

# "This is going to be a big favor, and I need it done ASAP."

*What She Says:*

# "No rush, whenever you get to it."

*What She Really Means:*

# "I need it done immediately, but I'm pretending to be laid-back."

*What She Says:*

**"You know what? Forget it."**

*What She Really Means:*

**"I'm giving you one last chance to fix this, or it's a big deal."**

*What She Says:*

**"I'll get over it."**

*What She Really Means:*

**"I'll remember this forever, and you're not off the hook."**

# "I'm just kidding!"

*What She Really Means:*

# "I'm half-serious, and you should take a hint."

Printed in Great Britain
by Amazon

55438955R00030